KIAC

FEB -- 2018

KNITTING FROM THE NORTH

———

Hilary runs her knitwear company from her studio in Orkney, Scotland. Since 2011 she has been designing winter accessories—hats, mittens, and scarves—and sending them out to independent boutiques, department stores, and customers all over the world from London to Tokyo.

KNITTING FROM THE NORTH

Original Designs Inspired by
Nordic and Fair Isle Knitting Traditions

Hilary Grant

Photography by Caro Weiss
and Kyle Books

Boulder 2016

Roost Books
An imprint of Shambhala Publications, Inc.
4720 Walnut Street, Boulder, Colorado 80301
roostbooks.com

ISBN: 978-1-61180-388-4

Designer: Graphical House
Photographer: Caro Weiss
Illustrator: Kuo Kang Chen
Make-up Artist: Sharon Stephen
Project Editor: Sophie Allen
Technical Editor: Elly Doyle
Editorial Assistant: Hannah Coughlin
Production: Nic Jones, Gemma John and Lisa Pinnell

9 8 7 6 5 4 3 2

First published in Great Britain by Kyle Books in 2016

Printed and bound in China by C&C Offset Printing Co., Ltd.

Distributed in the United States by Penguin Random House LLC and in Canada by Random
House of Canada Ltd

Library of Congress Cataloging-in-Publication Data
Names: Grant, Hilary, author. | Weiss, Caro, photographer (expression)
Title: Knitting from the North: original designs inspired by Nordic and Fair
Isle knitting traditions / Hilary Grant; photography by Caro Weiss.
Description: First U.S. edition. | Boulder: Roost Books, 2016.
Identifiers: LCCN 2016027142 | ISBN 9781611803884 (pbk.: acid-free paper)
Subjects: LCSH: Knitting—Scandinavia—Patterns. | Knitting—Scotland—Fair Isle—Patterns.
Classification: LCC TT819.S26 G73 2016 | DDC 746.43/209411—dc23
LC record available at https://lccn.loc.gov/2016027142

CONTENTS

INTRODUCTION

My studio window looks out onto a large natural harbor, sheltered on all sides by
a group of islands that are huddled amid the wild stretch of ocean where the North
Sea meets the Atlantic. It's a place where cultures meet, too—a brackish interweaving
of Nordic and Scottish influences.

This part of the world is the home of Fair Isle knitting, with its inventive cheerful patterns
and vibrant use of color. It's not hard to imagine why, in the long dark winters of the
Northern Isles, such an aesthetic tradition might arise. A similar tradition is found across
the Nordic countries too—from Icelandic yokes to iconic Norwegian 2-color knits.

I am not a traditional knitter, but that aesthetic is nevertheless present in my work.
I, too, find myself gravitating towards bright, cheerful colors and boldly patterned
designs—they seem a necessary response to the winters here. And the rhythm and meter
of Fair Isle knitting remain a constant source of inspiration for me.

For this book, with the help of local hand knitters, I have adapted some of my most
popular machine-knit patterns and designs. Each of the 30 projects use the color-strand
technique, typical of Fair Isle and Nordic knitting—using two different-colored yarns in
each row. The book covers techniques such as knitting-in-the-round, double-knitting, and
shaping. Also in keeping with this tradition, the styles are simple, practical, and timeless.

Some of the projects in this book are small enough to fill an empty afternoon.
Others should keep you knitting for weeks. I hope you enjoy these patterns and that
in reading this book, you will get to know something of the place that inspired them.

TECHNIQUES, KNITWEAR CARE & ABBREVIATIONS

GENERAL NOTES

All patterns require a blunt tapestry needle to weave in yarn ends.

All patterns specify a particular needle size. If your gauge differs from the gauge that is given, adjust your needle size accordingly, particularly when changing from plain stockinette stitch to colorwork.

Yarns

All yarn used is *Jamieson's Shetland Spindrift,* which is a fingering-weight yarn. It is sold in 0.9-ounce balls with a length of approximately 115 yards per ball. There are websites that can help you find substitutes if you wish to use an alternative, but here are some ideas—please take note that the gauge swatch is extremely important if you use a substitute. The weight is referred to as "Fingering Weight" when looking for alternatives.

Rauma, Lamullgarn (93% match)
Malsen Og Mor, Shetland soft (91% match)
Grant Creek Yarns, Cushy Merino 2-Ply (90% match)
Susan Crawford, Fenella 2-ply (90% match)
Sundara Yarn, Fingering Merino (89% match)

Waste Yarn

This is a smooth cotton yarn, ideally in the same weight or ply as the yarn you are using throughout your project. It helps if your waste yarn has a smooth handle and a contrasting color to your main color, as it will be easier to unravel when grafting ends together.

Gauge

Gauge refers to the number of stitches and rows that make up a 4-inch square. It is important to knit a gauge swatch before starting your project to ensure that your garment or accessory will fit correctly.

Color Knitting

In color knitting, two strands of color are worked in a single row. When working two strands of yarn, it is important to keep an eye on your gauge, as different patterns can end up worked tighter or looser than the instructions specify.

Cast-On

Make a slipknot. This is your first stitch. Place on the end of the left-hand needle and knit into the stitch. Place the stitch back on the left-hand needle and repeat the process until you have the number of stitches required per the instructions.

Provisional (Invisible) Cast-On

You will need 1 knitting needle and 1 crochet hook. Create a loose slipknot on your crochet hook. With the knitting needle in your left hand, take hold of the tail end of yarn with your left-hand fingers. Holding the crochet hook in your right hand, cross over the knitting needle. Take the working end of the yarn around the back and use the crochet hook to pull the yarn through the loop, That gives you 1 single cast-on stitch. Repeat the process for as many stitches as required.

Bind-Off

Knit 2 stitches. Take the first stitch on right-hand needle and pass it over the second stitch. Knit 1 stitch and pass the first stitch over the second stitch. Repeat this process until you have fully bound off. When the last stitch is on the right-hand needle, take the tail of the yarn and pull it through the last stitch to secure. Weave the tail into the reverse side of the knitting and trim the end of the tail.

Knit

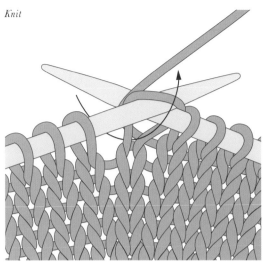

STITCHES

Knit

With your cast-on stitches on the left-hand needle, place the right-hand needle through the first stitch, entering the stitch from front to back (the needle points away from you). Wrap the yarn around the right-hand needle in an counterclockwise direction and with the same needle pull the yarn through so that you create a new stitch, which is now on the right-hand needle. Repeat this process.

Purl

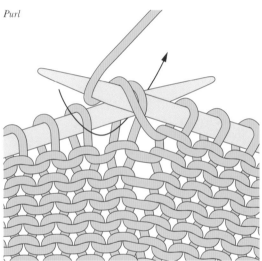

Purl

Instead of the right-hand needle entering the stitches from front to back, the needle enters from back to front (the needle points toward you). Wrap the yarn around the right-hand needle in a clockwise direction, pushing the yarn through the stitch to create a new one, which is now on the right-hand needle.

Make One

Work to the place where the increase is to be made. Insert the left needle from front to back into the horizontal strand between the two stitches: Knit the stitch through the back loop as shown. On the purl side, insert the needle from front to back and then purl the stitch through the back loop.

Make One

Stockinette Stitch

Work one row in knit and the following row in purl and repeat to create a fabric that has a smooth front. This is usually referred to as the "right" side of the knitting. When working in rounds, knit every round.

Double Knitting

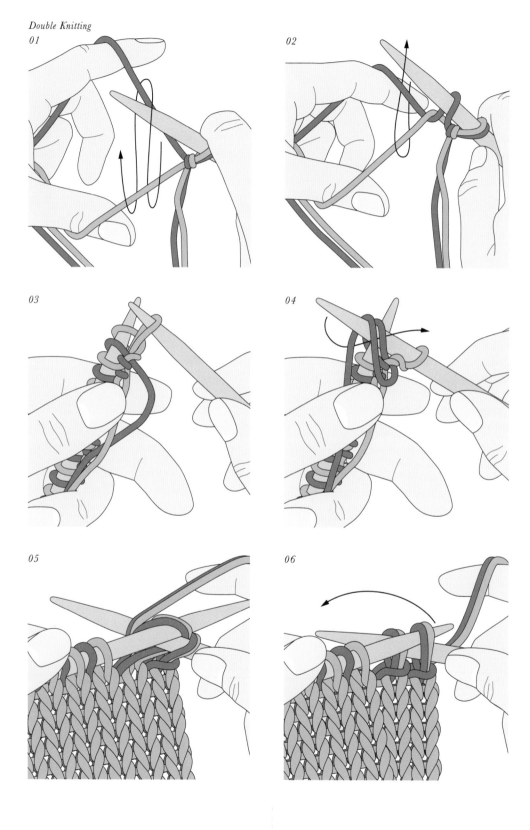

01

02

03

04

05

06

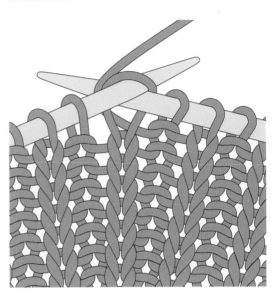

Double Knitting

This technique creates a fabric that has stockinette stitch on both sides. Both sides of the row are worked simultaneously. On the first row, work Color 1 as knit and Color 2 as purl. On the next row, you work Color 1 as purl and Color 2 as knit. Repeat. As you work each stitch, you must bring both yarns to either the front or the back of the knitting, but you are working only one yarn in each stitch.

Cast On for Double Knitting

Take both yarns, make a slipknot, and place on the left-hand needle. Pay attention to the order of the yarns. You will be casting on each yarn alternately. Color 1 is the first color on the needle. Hold the needle in your right hand. With your left hand you will be holding the yarns, keeping them separate with thumb and forefinger. Color 1 should be held by the forefinger and Color 2 by the thumb.

Bring the needle toward you over and under Color 2, away from you and over Color 1, then toward you under Color 2 again. That gives you one stitch in Color 1.

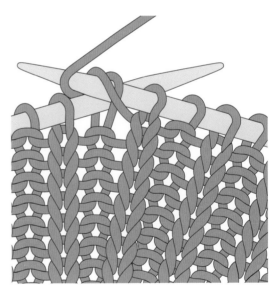

Bring the needle behind both yarns, away from you. Bring the needle under Color 2 and over. Bring the needle under Color 1 and over it. That gives you one stitch in Color 2.

For an item that is 10 stitches wide, you would cast on 10 stitches of each color (20 stitches total).

Bind Off for Double Knitting

To bind off, holding both yarns together, work the first knit-purl stitches together and then work the next knit-purl stitches together. Pass the first stitch over the second as you would for a regular bind-off.

Fisherman's Rib

Fisherman's rib is always worked over an even number of stitches. It involves working 1 stitch as a purl and working 1 stitch below as knit, allowing the stitch above to drop. The process is repeated to the end of the row. When there is a knit stitch at the beginning of a row, the top stitch is worked, instead of working into the stitch below. It creates a very full, stretchy fabric. Half Fisherman's Rib is used on page 104.

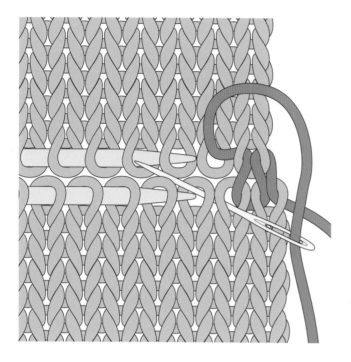

MAKING UP

Grafting or Kitchener Stitch

This is a method to join two pieces of knitting together.
It essentially involves sewing a row of knitting between two
raw or live ends.

Lay both pieces on a flat surface so that the knit side is facing
up and the raw ends/stitches are facing each other.
Thread your tapestry needle with the MC yarn.

Insert the needle purlwise into the first stitch on the lower
piece, then knitwise into the first stitch on the upper piece.
Pull the yarn through, working to maintain the same gauge
as the rest of your knitting.

*Insert the needle knitwise into the first stitch on the lower
piece again and pull the yarn through.

Insert the needle purlwise into the next stitch on the lower
piece and pull the yarn through.

Insert the needle purlwise into the first stitch on the upper
piece and pull the yarn through.

Insert the needle knitwise into the next stitch on the upper
piece and pull the yarn through.*

Repeat from * to * until you reach the end of the row.

Mattress Stitch

This is a method of joining two side seams together.
It gives you an invisible finish between the two seams.
Unlike Kitchener stitch, you work the yarn between
the stitches instead of through them. The thread is drawn
underneath the "bar," which is the stitch that runs behind
the V-shaped stitch of the right side.

With the knit-side of the piece facing you, lay the sides
to be joined next to each other, ensuring that the rows
are lined up as accurately as possible. You will be working
between these end courses of stitches to join them.
Seam the stitches, working one stitch in from the outside
edge, from one side to the other.

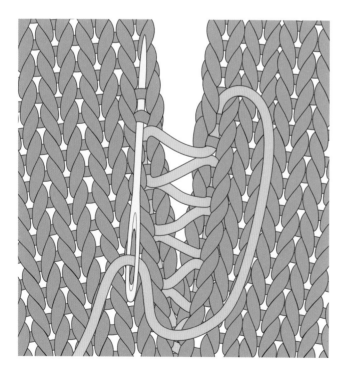

Half-Twist

A half-twist is required to create the twisted effect in the short cowls. If you lay your cowl on a flat surface, twist one end once so that the side that was facing you now faces the table. Then join using the technique specified in the pattern.

FINISHING

Daisy Chain

This method is similar to running a thread through a stitch, but it achieves a more even and secure gather. Take a tapestry needle threaded with a strong thread (topstitch thread plied twice) and sew onto the end of the knitting you wish to gather. Weave the needle in and out of the knitting at 1-inch intervals and pull tightly to gather. You will see a daisylike shape made. Then weave the needle in and out of the other ends (which look like tips of petals), pull tightly to gather, and secure with a couple of stitches.

Blocking

Blocking is manipulating your knitting into shape by wetting the item, shaping and securing it onto a surface using pins, and then setting it in shape either by allowing it to dry naturally or by drying it under the heat of an iron.

You can do this right on your ironing board, or you can use special blocking mats if you need a larger surface for blocking a garment. Always check the washing and pressing instructions on your yarn ball band for temperature and care guidance before blocking or pressing your garment.

Blocking A Round Beret

Soak the beret in cold water for 15 minutes. You can add a small amount of fabric softener or no-rinse wool wash if you desire. Insert a round plate that is slightly larger than the circumference of your hat and position the beret so that the center of the crown is lined up with the center of the plate. Ensure that the beret is stretched evenly over the plate and allow it to dry in a warm, dry place (but not next to a direct heat source, as this may shrink your beret) on top of a towel or drying rack.

Daisy Chain

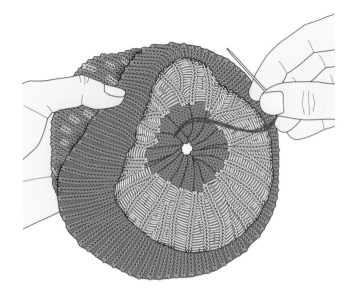

Blocking

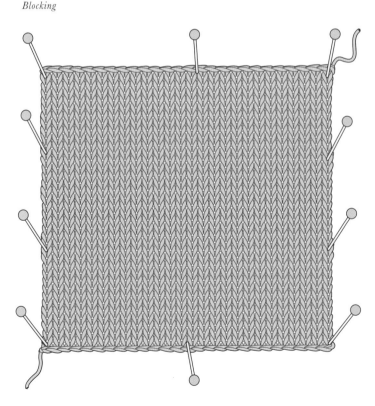

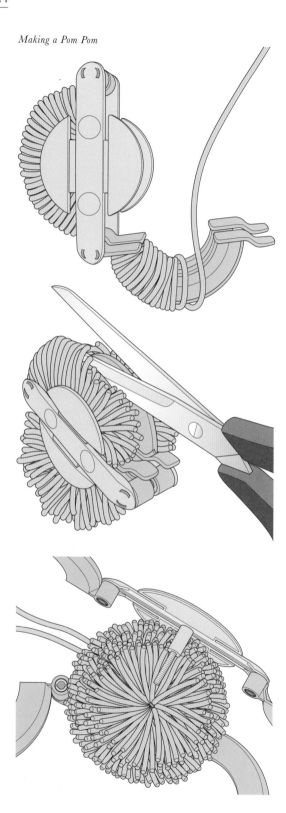

Making a Pom Pom

Making a Pom-Pom

You will need:
Pom-pom Maker: 1½-in diameter
½ ball of *Jamieson's Shetland Spindrift*

The secret to making a good pom-pom is having a very dense pile that is trimmed very well. Using your pom-pom maker of choice, wrap the yarn around each side according to the instructions provided. Use topstitch thread plied three or four times to tie your pom-pom. Holding each end of the topstitch thread, wrap one end around 3 times, creating a triple knot before pulling tightly to ensure that the yarns are pulled in well and held securely.

With a pair of sharp scissors, trim your pom-pom (being careful not to cut off the threads, as you will use them to attach the pom-pom to the hat), turning it constantly to ensure that it doesn't end up lopsided. Have patience with this part and you will have a beautifully round pom-pom.

Attaching the Pom-Pom

To attach your pom-pom to your hat, separate the threads into two groups. Working from the right side of your knitting, sew one group just to the right of the center of the crown, or where your hat has been gathered. Sew the other group just to the left of the center of the crown. Open up your hat and tie a triple knot, which will be concealed within the inside of the hat. Tie another triple knot to be certain. Before trimming the ends, gently tug the pom-pom to ensure that it is secure and not slack. Trim the ends of the thread inside the hat.

Adding Mitten Strings

Measure the length of the arms, across the shoulders. This will determine how long your mitten strings need to be. Using a Knitting Dolly, knit a length of cord, using MC yarn. Use instructions specific to the brand/make of your knitting dolly. Ensure you have a generous length rather than too little. If you have too much length you can always knot the cord to shorten it. Secure the ends of the mitten cord to the inside cuff using the MC yarn and a tapestry needle.

KNITWEAR CARE

Taking care of your knitwear is tremendously worthwhile because it will look, feel, smell, and fit well for a long, long time. If you have a knitted garment that has stretched out a bit or has lost its luster, a gentle hand-wash and press is usually enough to bring it back to its former glory. I cannot recommend this enough.

I like to have a big hand-wash session two or three times a year where I'll wash everything from cashmere cardigans and wool throws to all my lambswool accessories. I recommend hand-washing particularly for those accessories that come in close contact with your face, such as hats and mittens, which end up getting grubby after a full winter season of makeup, pollution, and perspiration.

Moths

In most cases you won't see any sign of moths until you unfold your favorite sweater when summer is over only to find holes dotted all over it. That is why you need to be really vigilant when it comes to storing and caring for your knitwear.

I don't like to store my knitwear tucked away in my closet; instead, I keep it stored with the rest of my clothing so it gets a bit of fresh air and sunlight every morning. If you use wicker baskets to store your knitwear, wash them in the bathtub every 6 months. Storing the most expensive and loved items in plastic bags in the freezer ensures that no living thing will be able to eat away at your most expensive and loved knitwear.

Cedar also acts as a good deterrent. If you have access to a local woodworker, ask if they will sell you some cedar offcuts. Cut them into small pieces, sand off all the rough edges, and give them a wipe before placing them in your drawer. Or you can drill a hole through one end, thread a length of waxed cord through, and hang it up in your closet. Sand the surface occasionally to revive the wood and release the smell.

How To Wash Your Knitwear

There are many options for washing and caring for delicate knitwear and garments. I have tried quite a few, and I tend to favor the eco-friendly options, as they don't smell too overpowering and are less damaging to the environment. The no-rinse brands are good if you are short on time.

You will need detergent suitable for wool; rubber gloves if you have sensitive skin; two or three large clean, dry towels; and a large, clean sink.

Fill a clean sink with lukewarm water (it should never feel hot to the skin).

Use about a teaspoon of detergent (or as instructed on the detergent label) and swish it around so that it disperses in the water.

Place your knitted item in the water and gently press it down so that it becomes fully submerged and saturated. Don't rub your knitwear. Leave it to soak for 5–10 minutes.

Drain all the water and press as much of the dirty water out of the knitting as you can.

Fill the sink with lukewarm water again and move the knitting around to rinse away all the suds and dirty water.

Again, drain the water and press all the water out of the knitting.

Place the knitting on a towel, roll up, and gently squeeze to remove all the water. Depending on the size of your garment, you might have to do this more than once and replace the soaked towel with a dry one.

Reshape the knitting on a fresh dry, flat towel and allow to dry away from direct heat.

Once your knitting has dried, use an iron to gently press it into shape. You might have to do a bit of reshaping again. Check the instructions on the yarn ball band or garment label regarding the iron heat setting.

ABBREVIATIONS

CC – contrast color

dpns – double-pointed needles

K – knit stitch

KFB – knit in front and back

K1b – Knit 1 below

K2tog – knit 2 stitches together

MC – main color

M1 – make 1 stitch by lifting horizontal strand between stitches and knitting into back of it.

P – purl stitch

P1b – Purl 1 below

P2tog – purl 2 stitches together

sl1 – slip 1 stitch without knitting it

sl1-k1-psso – slip 1 stitch to right-hand needle, knit next stitch, pass slipped stitch over knitted stitch

sl2-k1-psso – slip 2 stitches together to right-hand needle, knit next stitch, pass 2 slipped stitches over knitted stitch

ssk – slip slip knit

st(s) – stitch(es)

St st – stockinette stitch

BEACON POM HAT

This hat is worked in the round in K2, P2 rib. This is a slouchy style,
but it can be worn with a turned-up cuff for warmer ears and a neater fit.
The hat and the pom pom look particularly striking, like a bright beacon,
when created in a single colored yarn.

Finished Size
Circumference: 17¾ in, to be
worn with up to 4 in negative ease
Length: 8½ in

Yarn
Jamieson's Shetland Spindrift
      1 ball *Poppy* (MC)
Heavy cotton thread

Needles & Notions
US 2 (2.75mm) circular needle
16 in long and dpns
Stitch marker

Gauge
32 sts × 38 rows = 4 × 4 in over
unstretched rib

INSTRUCTIONS

Cast on 144 sts and place marker. Join to work in the round.

Work in K2, P2 rib for 8¼ in or to desired length.

Next round: [K2tog, P2] to end of round.
Next round: [K1, P2tog] to end of round.
Next round: [K1, P1] to end of round.

Bind off.

FINISHING

Thread a tapestry needle with heavy cotton thread.
Daisy chain around top of hat, weave in ends, and block.
Make pom-pom (see Techniques on page 14) and sew onto
top of hat.

FISHERMAN'S RIB
FINGERLESS MITTENS

This is a simple project to introduce you to working the
Fisherman's Rib stitch. It is dense yet stretchy, which ensures a snug
but comfortable fit. Use mattress stitch to seam the mittens together.

Finished Size
Circumference: 7⅛ in when
unstretched (will fit up to 8⅝ in
comfortably)
Height: 5½ in

Yarn
Jamieson's Shetland Spindrift
                    2 balls *Cobalt*

Needles & Notions
Pair US 2 (2.75mm) straight
needles

Gauge
27 sts × 32 rows = 4 × 4 in over
Fisherman's Rib

INSTRUCTIONS
Cast on 56 sts, leaving a tail long enough to use for
sewing up.

Work three rows in St st.

Begin Fisherman's Rib Pattern
Row 1: [K1, P1] across row.
Row 2: [K1b, P1] across row.

Repeat these two rows until work measures 5⅜ in or
desired length.

Work three rows in St st. Bind off. Break yarn,
leaving a tail long enough to use for sewing up.

FINISHING
Sew side seams together using mattress stitch, leaving a
1⅜-in gap (or longer if required) for the thumb 2¾ in up from
the bottom.
Weave in ends and block (see page 13).

ARROW POM HAT

My arrow pattern has a bold, simple repeat, making it a good
introduction to color knitting. I have found that it's best worked
in monochrome, or in a strong color with a white contrast,
for a classic Nordic look. This hat is worked in the round and
then simply gathered at the crown.

Finished Size
Circumference: 19⅝ in, to be worn
with up to 5½ in negative ease
Length: 8⅝ in

Yarn
Jamieson's Shetland Spindrift
       1 ball *Charcoal* (MC)
       1 ball *Natural White* (CC)

Needles and Notions
US 2 (3mm) circular needle
16 in long
US 3 (3.25mm) circular needle
16 in long
Stitch marker

Gauge
28 sts × 32 rows = 4 × 4 in over
colorwork using larger needle

Note
For each round, read chart from
right to left, knit every round.

INSTRUCTIONS

Using MC and smaller needle, cast on 140 sts.
Place marker and join to work in the round,
being careful not to twist.

Work 11 rounds of K1, P1 rib.

Change to larger needle.
Knit one round.

Join in CC. Following chart, work 20-st repeat 7 times across
round. Complete chart to end round 51. Break CC.

K eight rounds in MC.

Bind off.

FINISHING

Daisy chain around top of hat. Weave in ends.
Make a pom-pom in CC (see Techniques on page 14)
and sew onto top of hat.

Chart
MC   *White Square*
CC   *Grey Square*

ARROW CUFFS

These little cuffs are worked in the round and are quick to knit,
so they make a good project for an idle afternoon or evening.
These are brilliant for windy days. They stop drafts from coming up
your jacket sleeves, and they look lovely layered
over the cuffs of a chunky sweater.

Finished Size
Length: 3⅞ in
Circumference: 7⅞ in

Yarn
Jamieson's Shetland Spindrift
　　　1 ball *Old Gold* (MC)
　　　1 ball *Natural White* (CC)

Needles & Notions
US 1 (2.25mm) dpns
US 2 (2.75mm) dpns
Stitch marker

Gauge
30 sts × 36 rows = 4 × 4 in over
colorwork using larger needles

Note
For each round, read chart from
right to left, knit every round.

INSTRUCTIONS

Using MC and smaller needles, cast on 60 sts.
Place marker and join to work in the round,
being careful not to twist.

Work eight rounds of K2, P2 rib.
Change to larger needles.
Next round: K.

Join in CC.
Following chart, work 10-st repeat 6 times across round and
complete chart to end round 22.

Next round: Work one round in MC.
Change to smaller needles.
Work eight rounds of K2, P2 rib.

Bind off.

FINISHING

Weave in ends and block.

Chart
MC   *White Square*
CC   *Grey Square*

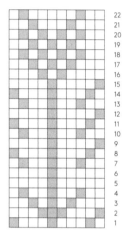

DOT DASH COWL

———

This cowl is worked in the round with a half-twist and then grafted
so that it has a seamless finish. Take your time with the grafting and try
to ensure that your stitches are as even as possible. I have used really
strong colors in this pattern—deep-sea blues, greens, and
oxide reds with a crisp white.

Finished Size

Circumference: 24½ in
Width: 5⅛ in

Yarn

Jamieson's Shetland Spindrift
  3 balls *Heron* (MC)
  1 ball *Ginger* (CC1)
  1 ball *Natural White* (CC2)
  1 ball *Aqua* (CC3)
  1 ball *Stonewash* (CC4)
  1 ball *Mermaid* (CC5)
Waste yarn

Needles & Notions

US 3 (3.25mm) circular needle
11⅞ in long
Stitch marker
Dpns in similar size to hold sts
for grafting

Gauge

30 sts × 32 rows = 4 × 4 in

Note

For each round, read charts from
right to left, knit every round.

INSTRUCTIONS

Using waste yarn and provisional method, cast on 80 sts. Place marker and join to work in the round, being careful not to twist.

Work through the various charts as follows, repeating each chart 20 times across the round.

1–12: Using MC and CC1, work Main A. (12 rounds)
13–24: Work Transition A, joining CC2 on third round. (12 rounds)
25–48: Using MC and CC2, work Main A twice. (12 rounds)
49–60: Work Transition B, joining CC3 on third round. (12 rounds)
61–84: Using MC and CC3, work Main A twice. (24 rounds)
85–96: Work Transition A, joining CC4 on third round. (12 rounds)
97–120: Using MC and CC4, work Main A twice. (24 rounds)
121–132: Work Transition B, joining CC5 on third round. (12 rounds)
133–156: Using MC and CC5, work Main A twice. (24 rounds)
157–168: Work Transition A, joining CC1 on third round. (12 rounds)
169–180: Using MC and CC1, work Main A once, omitting final round. (11 rounds)

FINISHING

Unravel the provisional cast-on and place the released sts on dpns. Lay your knitting flat on a table and fold so that there is a half-twist (see Techniques on page 13).
Graft the two ends together using MC.
Darn over the sts with CC so that the pattern continues all the way around the scarf.
Weave in ends and block.

Chart
MC   *White Square*
CC1   *Dark Grey Square*
CC2   *Light Grey Square*

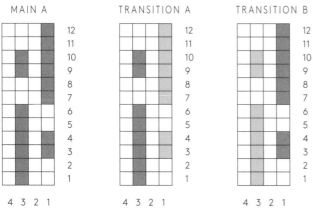

MAIN A   TRANSITION A   TRANSITION B

BARLEY FINGERLESS MITTENS

These fingerless mittens are worked in the round. They are quite short on the fingers, so they are well suited for when you need to be both warm and dexterous. This is another pattern that benefits from a crisp, bold colorway.

Finished Size
Circumference: 7⅞ in
Length: 6¼ in

Yarn
Jamieson's Shetland Spindrift
      1 ball *Verdigris* (MC)
      1 ball *Natural White* (CC)
Waste yarn

Needles & Notions
US 1 (2.25mm) dpns
US 2 (2.75mm) dpns
Stitch marker

Gauge
40 sts × 40 rows = 4 × 4 in over
colorwork using larger needles

Notes
For each round, read chart from
right to left, knit every round.

In rounds where there are blocks
of more than 5 sts of MC, twist
the yarns around each other at the
back every few stitches to prevent
long loops from forming.

INSTRUCTIONS, RIGHT
Using MC and smaller needles, cast on 80 sts. Place marker
and join to work in the round, being careful not to twist.

Work ten rounds of K2, P2 rib.
Change to larger needles.
Knit one round.

Join in CC.
Following chart, work 40-st repeat twice across round, to
end of Round 33.

Round 34: Work chart for 3 sts. K9 in waste yarn. Slip these
9 sts back onto left-hand needle, then complete round
following chart.

Complete chart to end Round 43.
Knit one round.
Change to smaller needles.
Work ten rounds of K2, P2 rib.

Bind off.

INSTRUCTIONS, LEFT
Work as for right to end of Round 33.

Round 34: Work chart for 28 sts. K9 in waste yarn. Slip these
9 sts back onto left-hand needle, then continue following
chart.
Continue working rest of round.

Complete as for right.

Chart
MC   *White Square*
CC   *Grey Square*

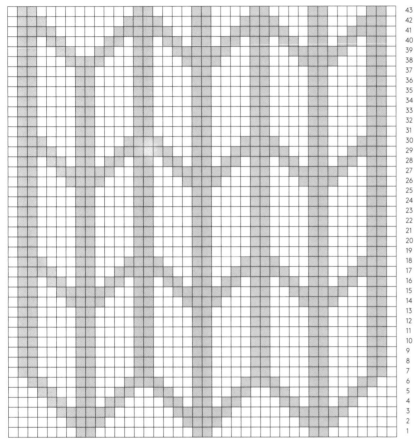

43
42
41
40
39
38
37
36
35
34
33
32
31
30
29
28
27
26
25
24
23
22
21
20
19
18
17
16
15
14
13
12
11
10
9
8
7
6
5
4
3
2
1

40 39 38 37 36 35 34 33 32 31 30 29 28 27 26 25 24 23 22 21 20 19 18 17 16 15 14 13 12 11 10 9 8 7 6 5 4 3 2 1

THUMBS
Using smaller needles, pick up the 9 sts both below and above the row of waste yarn—you will have 18 sts over 2 needles. Very carefully pull the waste yarn out, then divide the sts equally among 4 dpns.
Knit for 1⅛ in or to desired length.

Bind off.

FINISHING
Weave in ends, closing any small gaps left at base of thumb. Block.

ARROW CIRCLE SCARF

———

This circle scarf is worked flat and then the ends are grafted together. It will take a while to work through the pattern, but in the end you will have a brilliantly huge, warm scarf that can be worn in a multitude of ways.

Finished Size
Circumference: 59 in
Width: 13¾ in

Yarn
Jamieson's Shetland Spindrift
        7 balls *Charcoal* (MC)
        3 balls *Natural White* (CC)
Waste yarn

Needles & Notions
Pair US 2 (3mm) straight needles

Gauge
30 sts × 32 rows = 4 × 4 in

Note
When working from chart, odd
numbered rows are knit rows
and read from right to left. Even
numbered rows are purl rows, read
from left to right.

INSTRUCTIONS

Using waste yarn and provisional method, cast on 100 sts.
Using MC, purl one row.

Join in CC.
Beginning with a RS row and working in St st throughout,
following chart, work 20-st repeat 5 times across row.
Work through chart 8 times, work chart one final time to
end on Row 51 of chart (475 rows worked in total).
Break MC, leaving approximately a 50-in tail to graft the
ends.

FINISHING

Remove provisional cast-on and place sts on a knitting
needle. Graft the two ends using Kitchener stitch and MC.

Chart
MC   *White Square*
CC   *Grey Square*

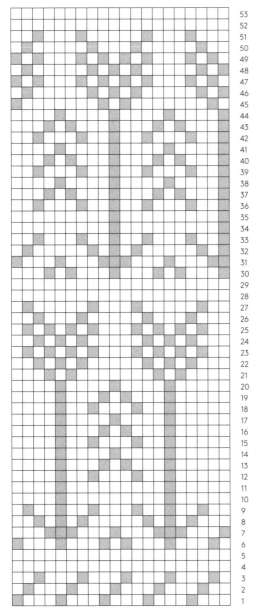

53
52
51
50
49
48
47
46
45
44
43
42
41
40
39
38
37
36
35
34
33
32
31
30
29
28
27
26
25
24
23
22
21
20
19
18
17
16
15
14
13
12
11
10
9
8
7
6
5
4
3
2
1

20 19 18 17 16 15 14 13 12 11 10 9 8 7 6 5 4 3 2 1

BARLEY TWIST HEADBAND

This headband is worked flat in double knitting and has a cable-style
twisted plait. The twist is worked by separating the knitting into
two cables, which are plaited and then joined back together.
See the Techniques section for more information
on double knitting (page 11).

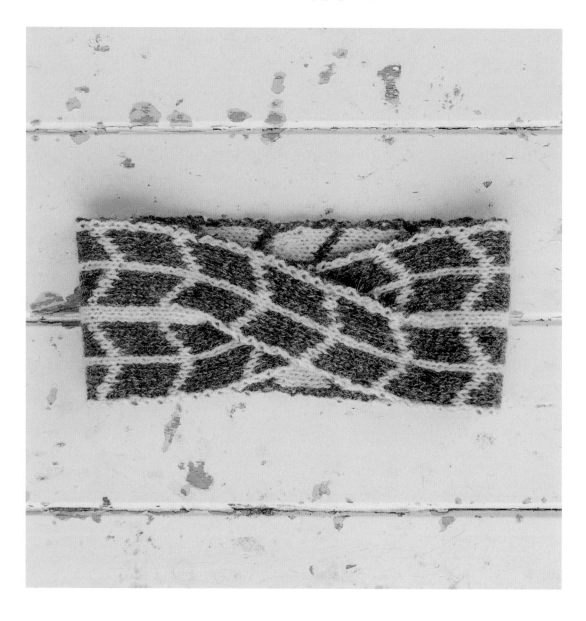

Finished Size
Circumference: 19⅝ in
Width: 3⅞ in

Yarn
Jamieson's Shetland Spindrift
    1 ball *Heron* (MC)
    1 ball *Natural White* (CC)
Waste yarn

Needles & Notions
Pair US 5 (3.75mm) straight
needles
US 5 (3.75mm) dpns
Stitch holders

Gauge
22 sts × 29 rows = 4 × 4 in

Notes
Each square on the chart
represents a pair of stitches, a knit
and a purl. For each square, knit
with the color shown on the chart,
then purl with the other color.
Before you knit, bring both yarns
to the back of the work, and then,
before you purl, bring both yarns
to the front of the work.

At the start of each row, twist the
yarns around each other once to
prevent the work from gaping at
the edge.

INSTRUCTIONS
Using waste yarn and provisional method, cast on 44 sts.
Using the double knitting method, work through the chart
for 55 rows.

Add the twist
From the next row you will be working over the first half of
the sts only. Slip the remaining half of the sts to a stitch
holder for ease of working. Continuing to use the double
knitting method, work 32 rows of the chart. Slip these sts to
a stitch holder. Break yarns, rejoin at start of
the remaining sts, and complete as for first half.
Cross the two halves once, as per the photo on page 50.

Join the two halves
Transfer all the sts to one needle. You will now work over
all the sts. Work 56 more rows of the chart. If you want to
shorten or length the headband here, finish one row short of
a full repeat of the chart.

FINISHING
Separate the front and back sides onto two needles.
Remove provisional cast-on and place the sts on a knitting
needle, separating the front and back sts. Using MC, graft
the two front sets of sts together. Repeat for the back sets.
Darn over the sts with CC so that the pattern continues all
the way around the headband. Weave in ends and block.

Chart
MC   *White Square*
CC   *Grey Square*

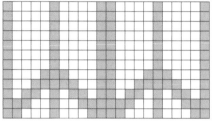

SAXON HAT

This pattern was inspired by a hand-painted stool that was made by and handed down through the family. The hat is knitted in the round and the shaping is done in a single color, so it's good for beginners. I always top my hats with a pom-pom, but the crown is shaped and very softly peaked, so it looks just as good without one.

Finished Size

Circumference: 20½ in, to be
worn with up to 2 in negative ease
Height: 9 in

Yarn

Jamieson's Shetland Spindrift
    1 ball *Heron* (MC)
    1 ball *Granite* (CC1)
    1 ball *Natural White* (CC2)

Needles & Notions

US 2 (2.75mm) circular needle
16 in long and dpns
Stitch markers

Gauge

28 sts × 32 rows = 4 × 4 in

Notes

For each round, read chart from
right to left, knit every round.

INSTRUCTIONS

Using MC, cast on 144 sts. Place marker and join to work
in the round, being careful not to twist.
Work 40 rounds of K2, P2 rib.
Knit three rounds.

Join in CC yarns.
Following chart, work 12-st, repeat 12 times across round.
Complete chart to end Round 28.
Break MC and CC1.

Knit 2 rounds.
Next round: [Place marker, K9] 16 times.

Next round: [K to 2 sts before marker, K2tog]
to end of round.
Next round: K.
Repeat these two rounds until 32 sts remain.

Next round: [K2tog] to end of round.
Next round: K.

Fasten off, leaving an 8-in tail.

FINISHING

Using a tapestry needle, draw tail through remaining
sts and pull tight. Weave in ends.

OPTIONAL: Make a pom-pom (see Techniques on page 14)
with CC1 and sew onto top of hat, ensuring that the pom-
pom conceals the gathered end.

Chart
MC   *Dark Grey Square*
CC1   *White Square*
CC2   *Light Grey Square*

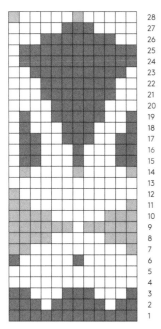

WEFT CUFFS

Like the Arrow Cuffs, these cuffs are worked in the round and offer warmth and comfort, but because there are three strands worked through, the knit is a little denser and therefore warmer. You can use the colorway I have suggested or make your own using tonal variations of one shade.

Finished Size
Circumference: 7⅞ in
Length: 4¾ in

Yarn
Jamieson's Shetland Spindrift
      1 ball *Mermaid* (MC)
      1 ball *Stonewash* (CC1)
      1 ball *Caspian* (CC2)
Waste yarn

Needles & Notions
US 1 (2.25mm) circular needle
9 in long
US 2 (2.75mm) circular needle
9 in long

Gauge
30 sts × 32 rows = 4 × 4 in over
colorwork using larger needles

Notes
Read chart from right to left.

INSTRUCTIONS

Using MC and smaller needle cast on 64 sts. Place marker and join to work in the round, being careful not to twist.

Work eight rounds of K2, P2 rib.
Change to larger needle.
Next round: K.

Join in CC yarns.
Following chart, work 8-st repeat 8 times across round.
Complete chart 6 times (24 chart rounds in total.)

Next round: K.
Work eight rounds of K2, P2 rib.

Bind off.

FINISHING
Weave in ends and block.

Chart
MC   *Light Grey Square*
CC1   *White Square*
CC2   *Dark Grey Square*

ICELANDIC FAUX TURTLENECK

The Icelandic pattern is one of my favorite designs. This turtleneck is worked in the round, before the back and front are separated and worked flat. It has a front and a back bib, which gives the impression of being a full sweater when worn under a coat. This is a neat and tidy piece to keep your neck and chest warm when you don't want to wear a bulky scarf.

Finished Size

Bib width: 8⅝ in
Bib height: 7½ in
Neck rib circumference: 13⅜ in
when unstretched

Yarn

Jamieson's Shetland Spindrift
      2 balls *Heron* (MC)
      1 ball *Ginger* (CC)

Needles & Notions

US 2 (2.75mm) circular needle
9 in long
Pair US 2 (2.75mm) straight
needles
Stitch marker

Gauge

27 sts × 35 rows = 4 × 4 in

Notes

When working from chart, odd
numbered rows are knit rows, read
from right to left. Even numbers
rows are purl rows, read from left
to right.

INSTRUCTIONS

Using MC and circular needle, cast on 144 sts. Place marker
and join to work in the round, being careful not to twist.

Neck

Work 44 rounds of K2, P2 rib.
Next round: [Bind off 6 sts, K2, P2, K58, P2, K2] twice.

You will now have two sections of 66 sts each.
One will be the front bib and the other the back bib—
both will be worked the same.

Transfer one of the groups of 66 sts to a straight needle.

Bib

Join in CC
Next row: K2, P2, K3, work chart, K2, P2, K2.
Next row: P2, K2, P3, work chart, P2, K2, P2.

Repeat these two rows until chart is complete. Break CC.
Work one row as established using MC only.

Work eight rows of K2, P2 rib, starting and ending with K2.
Repeat for second bib.

Bind off. Weave in ends.

FINISHING

Block after completing second bib.

Chart
MC   *White Square*
CC   *Grey Square*

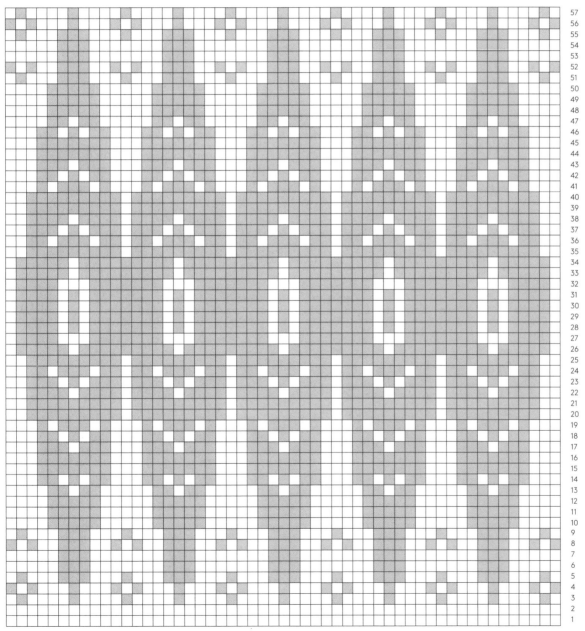

TIDE MITTENS

———

These are worked in the traditional, pointed Nordic style, which produces a
very flat mitten and an iconic profile. Make sure to twist your yarns so that
the longer strands are worked into the knitting instead of being left loose.

Finished Size
Circumference: 8¼ in
Length: 8⅝ in

Yarn
Jamieson's Shetland Spindrift
  1 ball *Heron* (MC)
  2 balls *Eggshell* (CC)
Waste yarn

Needles & Notions
US 1 (2.25mm) dpns
US 2 (2.75mm) dpns
Stitch markers

Gauge
36 sts × 40 rows = 4 × 4 in over
colorwork using larger needles

Notes
For each round, read chart from
right to left, knit every round.

When there are blocks of more
than 5 stitches of MC, twist the
yarns around each other at the
back every few stitches to prevent
long loops from forming.

INSTRUCTIONS

RIGHT MITTEN
Using smaller needles and MC, cast on 74 sts.
Work ten rounds of K1, P1 rib.

Change to larger needles.
Knit one round.
Work chart to end of Round 24.

Round 25: Work 3 sts following chart. Using waste yarn,
K10. Slip these 10 sts back onto left-hand needle,
then continue following chart.

Complete the chart, beginning top shaping on Round 66
as shown. 22 sts remain.

Break yarn, leaving an 8-in tail. Graft sts using Kitchener
stitch.

THUMB
Using smaller needles, pick up the 10 sts both below
and above the row of waste yarn—you will have
20 sts over 2 needles. Very carefully pull the waste
yarn out, then divide the sts equally among 4 dpns.

Knit for 2 in or to desired length.

Next round: [Ssk, K6, K2tog] twice.
Next round: [Ssk, K4, K2tog] twice.
Next round: [Ssk, K2, K2tog] twice.
8 sts remain.

Chart
MC   *Grey Square*
CC   *White Square*
/   *K2tog (knit 2 together)*
\   *SSK (slip slip knit)*

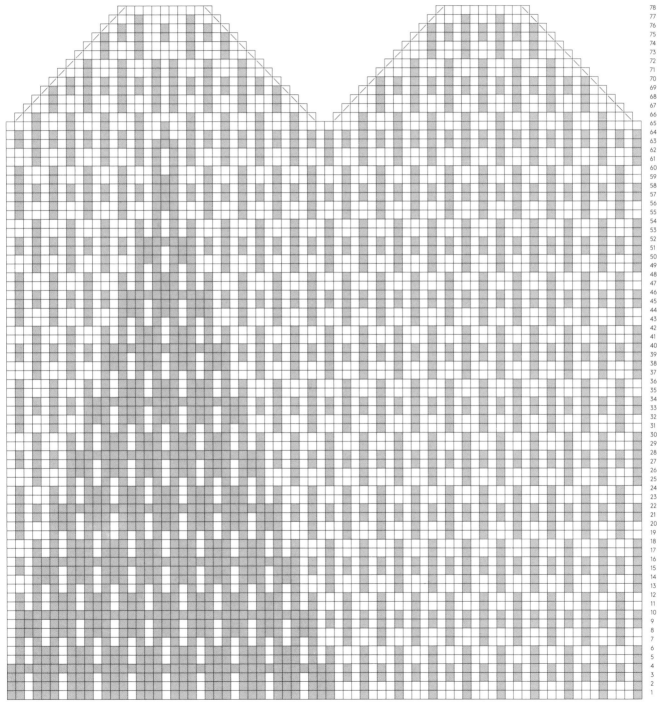

Break yarn, leaving an 8-in tail, and graft sts using Kitchener stitch.

LEFT MITTEN
Work as for right to end of Round 24.
Round 25: Work 24 sts following chart. Using waste yarn, K10. Slip these 10 sts back onto left-hand needle, then continue following chart.

Complete as for right.

FINISHING
Weave in ends and block.

BARLEY TWIST COWL

This is a nice meditative project to work through. You can work a
gradient through the contrast color if you like, but I think that the
graphic and clean contrast gives it a fresh and modern Scandinavian feel.
It is knit in the round like a tube, twisted, and then grafted.

Finished Size
Circumference: 26 in
Width: 6¼ in

Yarn
Jamieson's Shetland Spindrift
  2 balls *Natural White* (MC)
  2 balls *Bottle Green* (CC)
Waste yarn

Needles & Notions
US 3 (3.25mm) circular needle
11⅞ in long
Stitch marker
Dpns in similar size to hold
stitches for grafting

Gauge
30 sts × 33 rows = 4 × 4 in

Note
For each round, read chart from
right to left, knit every round.

INSTRUCTIONS

Using waste yarn and provisional method, cast on 96 sts. Place marker and join to work in the round, being careful not to twist.

Join in CC.
Following chart, work 12-st repeat 8 times across round. Work chart 22 times, at end of the end of the final repeat, omit the last round (219 rounds in total). Break both yarns, leaving a long enough tail of MC to graft the ends.

FINISHING

Unravel the provisional cast-on and place the released sts on dpns. Lay your knitting flat on a table and fold so that there is a half-twist (see Techniques on page 10).

Graft the two ends using tail of MC.

Darn over the sts with CC so that the pattern continues all the way around the scarf.

Weave in ends and block.

Chart
MC   *White Square*
CC   *Grey Square*

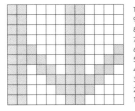

LOKI HAT

———

This hat is quite a close-fitting style, but it can be made larger
by increasing the number of repeats in the pattern. Knit in the round
with a shaped crown, this hat features my Loki pattern. The pattern will
pop even more if you choose yarns with a good amount of contrast in
either tone or color.

Finished Size

Circumference: 18⅛ in, to be worn with up to 3 in negative ease
Height: 7½ in

Yarn

Jamieson's Shetland Spindrift
　　　1 ball *Cornfield* (MC)
　　　1 ball *Natural White* (CC)
Heavy cotton thread

Needles & Notions

US 1 (2.25mm) circular needle 16 in long
US 2 (2.75mm) circular needle 16 in long and dpns
Stitch marker

Gauge

34 sts and 38 rows = 4 × 4 in

Notes

For each round, read chart from right to left, knit every round.

INSTRUCTIONS

Using smaller needle and MC, cast on 152 sts. Place marker and join to work in the round, being careful not to twist. Work ten rounds of K2, P2 rib.

Change to larger needles.
Next round: [K75, kfb] twice. (154 sts)

Join in CC.
Following chart, work 14-st repeat 11 times across round, beginning decreasing on Round 36. Complete the chart (67 rounds in total).

FINISHING

Bind off and daisy chain around the remaining 11 sts with heavy cotton thread of a similar color to your hat. Weave in ends.

Chart
MC   *Grey Square*
CC   *White Square*
/   *K2tog (knit 2 together)*
\   *SSK (slip slip knit)*

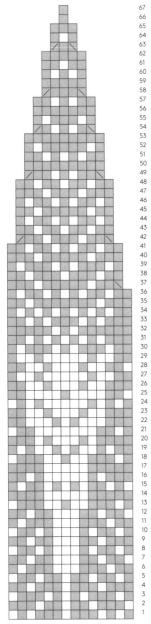

ICELANDIC MITTENS

These mittens have a traditional boxy profile. The ribbed cuffs are short,
but you can extend them if you would like a snugger fit around the wrists.
This pattern is worked in the round in a rich oxide red and
a crisp natural white.

Finished Size
Circumference: 8¼ in
Length: 8⅛ in

Yarn
Jamieson's Shetland Spindrift
       2 balls *Ginger* (**MC**)
        1 ball *Natural White* (**CC**)
Waste yarn

Needles & Notions
US 1 (2.25mm) dpns
US 1 (2.5mm) dpns
Stitch marker

Gauge
36 sts × 40 rows = 4 × 4 in over
colorwork using larger needles

Note
For each round, read chart from
right to left, knit every round.

INSTRUCTIONS

RIGHT MITTEN
Using MC and smaller needles, cast on 72 sts. Place marker and join to work in the round, being careful not to twist.

Work 12 rounds of K2, P2 rib.
Change to larger needles.
Next round: K.

Join in CC.
Following chart, work 36-st repeat twice until end of Round 23.
Round 24: Work 3 sts following chart. Using waste yarn, K10. Slip these 10 sts back onto left-hand needle, then continue following chart.

Complete the chart. Break CC.

Shaping the mitten top
Next round: Slip marker, K1, ssk, K31, K2tog, place marker, K1, ssk, K31, K2tog.

Next round: [Slip marker, K1, ssk, knit until 2 sts before marker, K2tog] twice. 4 sts decreased.
Repeat last round until 32 sts remain.

Break yarn, leaving an 8-in tail.
Graft sts using Kitchener stitch.

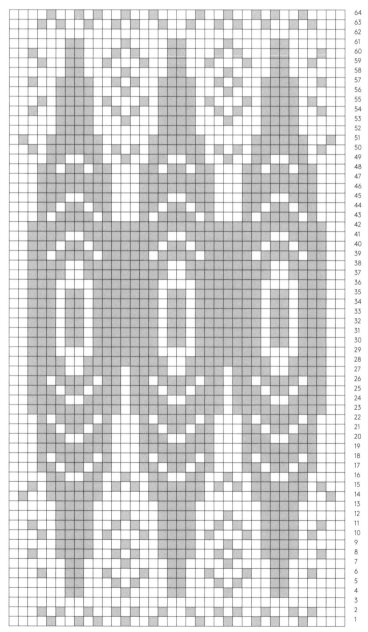

Thumb
Using smaller needles, pick up the 10 sts both below and above the row of waste yarn—you will have 20 sts over 2 needles. Very carefully pull the waste yarn out, then divide the sts equally among 4 dpns.
Knit for 2 in or to desired length.

Next round: [K1, ssk, K5, K2tog] twice.
Next round: [K1, ssk, K3, K2tog] twice.
Next round: [K1, ssk, K1, K2tog] twice.
8 sts remain.

Break yarn, leaving an 8-in tail. Graft sts using Kitchener stitch.

LEFT MITTEN
Work as for right to end of Round 23.
Round 24: Work 22 sts following chart. Using waste yarn, K10 sts. Slip these 10 sts back onto left-hand needle, then continue following chart.

Complete as for right mitten.

FINISHING
Weave in ends and block.

Chart
MC   *White Square*
CC   *Grey Square*

TIDE BERET

This hat is adapted from my Tide Scarf, which was part of my 2014 collection and uses the same motif as the Tide Mittens and very neutral colors. You can wear it as a slouchy beanie with the cuff turned up or as a little beret. This is a neat style, so if you want to make it bigger, you can increase by one horizontal repeat.

Finished Size

Circumference: 18⅛ in, to be worn with up to 2¾ in negative ease

Height: 9 in

Yarn

Jamieson's Shetland Spindrift

      1 ball *Natural White* (MC)

      1 ball *Heron* (CC)

Needles & Notions

US 1 (2.25mm) circular needle 16 in long

US 2 (2.75mm) circular needle 16 in long and dpns

Stitch marker

Gauge

32 sts × 42 rows = 4 × 4 in

Notes

For each round, read chart from right to left, knit every round.

When there is a long run between MC and CC, twist the yarns around each other at the back every few stitches to ensure that the long floats are secure and to maintain a consistent gauge.

INSTRUCTIONS

Using MC and smaller needle, cast on 144 sts. Place marker and join to work in the round, being careful not to twist.

Work in K2, P2 rib for 3½ in.
Change to larger needle.

Next round: [K3, M1] across round. (192 sts)

Join in CC.
Following chart, repeat 24-st repeat 8 times across round, working decreases from Round 27.
Complete chart.

FINISHING

Using a tapestry needle, thread tail through remaining sts and pull tight. Weave in ends.

Block over a form (see Techniques on page 13).

Chart
MC   *White Square*
CC   *Grey Square*
/   *K2tog (knit 2 together)*
\   *SSK (slip slip knit)*

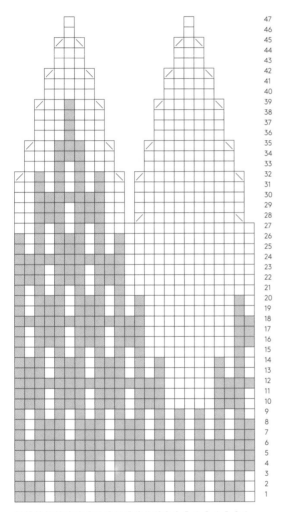

SAXON MITTENS

These mittens have a slightly looser gauge than the previous mittens, so there are fewer stitches. The style is more stretchy. The fingertips are shaped much like a hat would be when knit in the round, which gives the end of the mittens a softer shape. The looser gauge also allows the ribbed cuffs to have a little more spring and the mittens pull in at the wrist for a snug fit.

Finished Size
Fingertip to wrist: 7⅛ in
Length of cuff (unfolded): 3½ in
Circumference: 7⅞ in

Yarn
Jamieson's Shetland Spindrift
        2 balls *Caspian* (MC)
        1 ball *Heron* (CC1)
        1 ball *Granite* (CC2)
Waste yarn

Needles & Notions
US 1 (2.25mm) dpns
US 2 (2.75mm) dpns
Stitch marker

Gauge
32 sts & 42 rows = 4 × 4 in over
colorwork using larger needles

Notes
For each round, read chart from
right to left, knit every round.

INSTRUCTIONS

RIGHT MITTEN

Using CC1 and smaller needles, cast on 64 sts. Place marker and join to work in the round, being careful not to twist.

Work 40 rounds K2, P2 rib.
Change to larger needles.
Next Round: [K31, KFB] twice. (66 sts)
Join in MC and work nine rounds in MC.

Join in CC2. Following chart, work 33-st repeat twice across round, to end Round 17.

Round 18: Work 3 sts following chart. Using waste yarn, knit 10 sts. Slip these 10 sts back onto left-hand needle, then continue following chart.

Complete to end Round 26.
Break off CC colors. Work 29 rounds in MC.

Chart
MC   *White Square*
CC1   *Dark Grey Square*
CC2   *Light Grey Square*

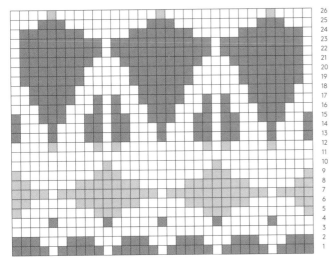

SHAPING THE FINGERTIPS

Round 66: [SSK, K6, SSK, K13, K2tog, K6 K2tog] twice.

Round 67: K.

Round 68: [SSK, K5, SSK, K11, K2tog, K5, K2tog] twice.

Round 69: K.

Round 70: [SSK, K4, SSK, K9, K2tog, K4, K2tog] twice.

Round 71: K.

Round 72: [SSK, K3, SSK, K7, K2tog, K3, K2tog] twice.

Round 73: K.

Round 74: [SSK, K2, SSK, K5, K2tog, K2, K2tog] twice.

Round 75: [SSK, K9, K2tog] twice.

Break yarn, leaving an 8-in tail. Graft using Kitchener stitch and weave in ends.

THUMB
Using smaller needles, pick up the 10 sts both below and above the row of waste yarn—you will have 20 sts over 2 needles. Very carefully pull the waste yarn out, then divide the sts equally among 4 dpns.

Using larger needles, knit 2 in or to desired length.

Next round: [SSK, K6, K2tog] twice.
Next round: [SSK, K4, K2tog] twice.
Next round: [SSK, K2, K2tog] twice.
8 sts remain.

Break yarn, leaving an 8-in tail, and graft using Kitchener stitch.

LEFT MITTEN
Work as for right to end of Round 17.
Round 18: Work 10 sts following chart.
Using waste yarn, K10. Slip these 10 sts back onto left-hand needle, then continue following chart.

Complete as for right.

FINISHING
Weave in ends and block. To add mitten strings, see page 14.

BARLEY HAT

This is a variation of my Pylon pattern that I designed in 2012. It's been adapted to hand knitting, so the strands taken across the back are shorter and therefore easier to work. This hat is worked in the round. The contrast colors are intended to create a gradient effect by using two shades of a single color.

Finished Size
Circumference: 19⅝ in, to be worn
with up to 3⅞ in negative ease
Height: 9 in

Yarn
Jamieson's Shetland Spindrift
       1 ball *Natural White* (MC)
       1 ball *Verdigris* (CC1)
       1 ball *Bottle* (CC2)
Heavy cotton thread

Needles & Notions
US 2 (2.75mm) circular needle
16 in long
Stitch marker

Gauge
28 sts × 32 rows = 4 × 4 in

Notes
For each round, read chart from
right to left, knit every round.

INSTRUCTIONS

Using MC, cast on 140 sts. Place marker and join
to work in the round, being careful not to twist.

Work ten rounds of K2, P2 rib.
Next round: K.

Join in CC.
Following chart, work 10-st repeat 14 times across round.
Complete chart to end Round 59.
Break off colors.

Bind off in MC.

FINISHING

Using a tapestry needle and heavy cotton thread
in a similar color to MC, daisy chain around top of hat.
Weave in ends and block.

Make a pom-pom in CC (see Techniques on page 14) and
sew onto top of hat, ensuring that the pom-pom conceals
the gathered end and is secured tightly.

Chart
MC   *White Square*
CC1   *Light Grey Square*
CC2   *Dark Grey Square*

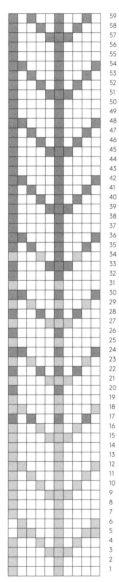

DOT DASH HEADBAND

This headband involves double knitting, which is quite a challenging technique but is well worth persevering with. It involves working a knit stitch on both sides, making for a thick, stretchy, and fully reversible fabric—perfect for a headband.

Finished Size
Circumference: 20½ in
Width: 4¾ in

Yarn
Jamieson's Shetland Spindrift
  1 ball *Aqua* (**MC**)
  1 ball *Heron* (**CC**)
Waste yarn

Needles & Notions
Pair US 5 (3.75mm) straight
needles
Pair US 2 (3mm) straight needles

Gauge
Headband: 23 sts × 27 rows =
4 × 4 in
Knot tube: 26 sts × 36 rows =
4 × 4 in

Note
Each square on the chart
represents a pair of stitches: a knit
and a purl. For each square, knit
with the color shown on the chart,
then purl with the other color.
Before you knit, bring both yarns
to the back of the work, then
before you purl, bring both yarns
to the front of the work.

At the start of each row, the yarns
should be twisted around each
other once to prevent the work
from gaping at the edges.

INSTRUCTIONS

HEADBAND
In the chart, each square represents both a knit and
a purl stitch. Twist the yarns around each other at
the start of every row to ensure that the edges fit together
without gaping.

With both MC and CC held together and using larger
needles, cast on 27 sts.

Following chart, work across the row.
Complete chart 9 times (126 rows worked in total). If you
want a larger or smaller headband, work more or fewer
repeats of the chart, remembering that you will need more
yarn if making it larger.

To bind off, holding both yarns together, knit the
first knit-purl pair of sts together, and then knit the next
knit-purl pair together. Then pass the first stitch over the
second as you would for a regular bind-off. Continue in this
manner to complete the bind-off.

KNOT TUBE
The knot will be knit in single knit. It's important that the
knot isn't as bulky, as you want it to pull in the headband
piece and not create too much thickness at the top of the
head.

Using waste yarn, smaller needles, and provisional method,
cast on 20 sts. Using MC, work in St st for 4⅜ in.

Remove provisional cast-on and place sts on a knitting
needle. Graft the two ends using Kitchener stitch and MC.

Chart
MC   *White Square*
CC   *Grey Square*

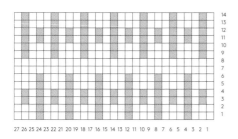

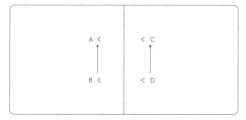

Grafted Seam

FINISHING

Block both pieces. The sides of the knot tube should curl in slightly. Thread the headband through the knot tube. Seam the two ends of the headband together.

Referring to the diagram, use a tapestry needle and MC to sew point A to B and point C to D securely.

This will create an even gathered effect at the center of your headband.

Pull the knot tube around so that it is centered over the seam of the headband.

FISHERMAN'S RIB
FAUX TURTLENECK

———

The fabric is created using Half Fisherman's Rib, which is dense yet stretchy and thus ideal for this style, fitting snugly around the neck and shoulders. It has been designed as an alternative to scarves for when you need an extra bit of warmth without the bulk.

Finished Size
Bib width: 8⅝ in
Bib length: 6¾ in
Neck rib circumference: 13⅜ in
when unstretched

Yarn
Jamieson's Shetland Spindrift
        3 balls *Natural White*

Needles & Notions
US 2 (2.75mm) circular needle
9 in long
Pair US 2 (2.75mm) straight
needles
Stitch marker

Gauge
27 sts × 32 rows = 4 × 4 in over
Half Fisherman's Rib

INSTRUCTIONS
Using circular needle, cast on 144 sts.

Work 43 rounds of P2, K2 rib (starting with P2 to match pattern further on in the work).

Next round: [Bind off 6 sts, K2, P2, K58, P2, K2] twice.

You will now have two sections of 66 sts each. One will be the front bib and the other the back bib. Both will be worked the same way.

Transfer one of the groups of 66 sts onto a straight needle.

Begin Half Fisherman's Rib Pattern
Row 1: K2, P2, K1, [P1b, K1] until 4 sts rem, P2, K2.
Row 2: P2, K2, P1, * [K1, P1] * rep * to * to end of row.

Repeat these two rows 33 times.
Work three rows of K2, P2 rib, starting and ending with K2.

Bind off.

Repeat with second group of sts for other bib.

FINISHING
Block after completing second bib and weave in ends.

WAVE FINGERLESS MITTENS

These mittens are long on both the fingers and the wrists, so they are
particularly warm. They are worked in the round, with
the thumbs worked in on waste yarn.

Finished Size
Circumference: 7⅞ in
Length: 10¼ in

Yarn
Jamieson's Shetland Spindrift
 2 balls *Aqua* (MC)
 1 ball *Natural White* (CC)
Waste yarn

Needles & Notions
US 2 (2.75mm) dpns
US 3 (3mm) dpns
Stitch marker

Gauge
29 sts × 38 rows = 4 × 4 in over
colorwork using larger needles

Notes
For each round, read chart from
right to left, knit every round.

INSTRUCTIONS

RIGHT MITTEN

Using MC and smaller needles, cast on 56 sts. Place marker and join to work in the round, being careful not to twist.

Work 30 rounds of K2, P2 rib.
Change to larger needles.

Next 2 rounds: K.

You will have a plain vertical column of stitches separating the start and the end of the pattern repeat in every circular row.

Following chart, work 28-st, repeat until end of Round 37.

Round 38: Work 3 sts following chart. Using waste yarn, K8. Slip these 8 sts back onto left-hand needle, then continue following chart.

Complete the chart to end Round 56. Break CC.

Next 2 rounds: K.

Change to smaller needles.
Work ten rounds of K2, P2 rib.

Bind off.

Chart
MC   *Grey Square*
CC   *White Square*

LEFT MITTEN

Work as for right to end of Round 37.

Round 38: Work 18 sts following chart. Using waste yarn, K8. Slip these 8 sts back onto left-hand needle, then continue following chart.

Complete as for right.

THUMBS

Using smaller needles, pick up the 8 sts both below and above the row of waste yarn—you will have 16 sts over 2 needles.

Very carefully pull the waste yarn out, then divide the sts equally among 4 dpns.

Work for 1⅛ in or to desired length.

Bind off.

FINISHING

Weave in ends, closing any small gaps left at base of thumb. Block.

ICELANDIC HAT

This design is influenced by the structured motifs of Icelandic sweater yokes.
I created it back in 2012 when I had just moved to Orkney and was really inspired
by the knitting from Scandinavian and Nordic countries. The hat is worked in the round
and shaped toward the crown. I think it looks best in classic Nordic colors—
oxide red, indigo, or black—with a white contrast.

Finished Size

Circumference: 22 in, to be worn with up to 2 in negative ease
Height: 8⅝ in, including unfolded ribbed brim

Yarn

Jamieson's Shetland Spindrift
         1 ball *Prussian* (MC)
         1 ball *Natural White* (CC)
Waste yarn
Heavy cotton thread

Needles & Notions

US 2 (2.75mm) circular needle
16 in long and dpns
Stitch marker

Gauge

30 sts × 32 rows = 4 × 4 in over colorwork.

Notes

For each round, read chart from right to left, knit every round.

INSTRUCTIONS

Using MC, cast on 160 sts. Place marker and join to work in the round, being careful not to twist.

Work in K2, P2 rib for 3½ in.
Knit two rounds.

Join in CC.
Following chart, work 10-st repeat 16 times across round.
Complete chart, working decreases from Round 21, to end Round 43.

Using CC, knit one round.
Next round: K2tog 16 times.
Bind off remaining sts.

FINISHING

Using a tapestry needle and heavy cotton thread in a similar color to MC, daisy chain around top of hat.

Make a pom-pom (see Techniques on page 14) and sew onto top of hat, ensuring that the pom-pom conceals the gathered end and is secured tightly. Weave in ends and block.

Chart
MC   *White Square*
CC   *Grey Square*
/   *K2tog (knit 2 together)*
\\   *SSK (slip slip knit)*

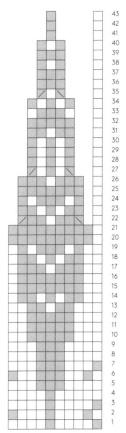

LOKI CIRCLE SCARF

This circle scarf is a slightly shorter version of the other circle scarves. It has a large vertical repeat and is one of the more complicated patterns in this book, but the resulting effect is striking even from a distance. The scarf is worked flat so that there is enough drape for it to sit nicely on the shoulders. I've used a saturated yellow with a crisp natural white yarn for maximum impact, but the colors can always be substituted if you are little less bold with color.

Finished Size
Circumference: 47¼ in
Width: 7½ in

Yarn
Jamieson's Shetland Spindrift
        2 balls *Cornfield* (MC)
        2 balls *Natural White* (CC)
Waste yarn

Needles & Notions
Pair US 2 (3mm) straight needles

Gauge
29 sts × 3 = 4 × 4 in

Note
When working from the chart, odd numbered rows are knit rows and read from right to left. Even numbered rows are purl rows and read from left to right.

INSTRUCTIONS
Using provisional method and waste yarn, cast on 55 sts. Join in MC and CC.
Following chart, work 55-st pattern once, repeating chart 5 times, omitting the last row on the final repeat (359 rows in total).

FINISHING
Unravel the provisional cast-on and place the released sts on a knitting needle.

Graft the two ends using MC.

Darn over the sts with CC so that the pattern continues all the way around the scarf.

Weave in ends and block.

Chart
MC   *White Square*
CC   *Grey Square*

TRIANGLE GLOVES/MITTENS

This project has a number of different options for the top.
Due to the placement of the motif, the glove is worked flat
and then joined at the sides.

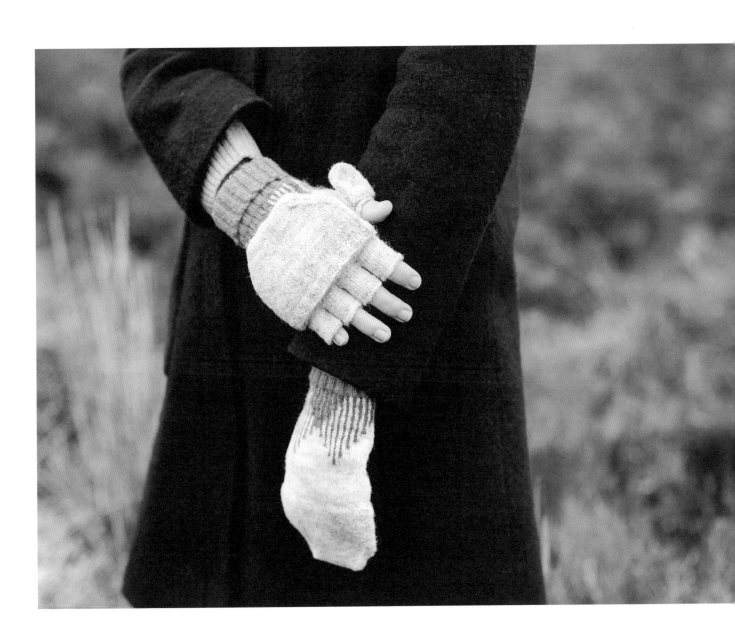

Finished Size
Palm circumference: 8¼ in

Yarn
Jamieson's Shetland Spindrift
    2 balls *Granite* (MC)
    1 ball *Sea Bright* (CC1)
    1 ball *Ginger* (CC2)

Needles & Notions
Pair US 1 (2.25mm) straight
needles
Pair US 2 (2.75mm) straight
needles
US 1 (2.25mm) dpns
Stitch holder
Stitch markers

Gauge
36 sts × 42 rows = 4 × 4 in
over colorwork using larger
needles

Notes
When working from the chart,
odd numbered rows are knit rows
and read from right to left. Even
numbered rows are purl rows and
read from left to right.

You will find it easier if you use
bobbins with small amounts of
yarn wound onto them for areas of
colorwork.

INSTRUCTIONS

SHORT-FINGERED GLOVES, RIGHT
Using CC1 and smaller needles, cast on 74 sts.

Row 1 (RS): K1, work K2, P2 rib to last stitch, K1.
Row 2 (WS): P1, work K2, P2 rib to last stitch, P1.
Repeat these two rows until work measures 3⅛ in,
ending with a WS row.

Change to larger needles.
Join in MC.

Next row: K1 MC, work across chart twice, K1 MC.
Next row: P1 MC, work across chart twice, P1 MC.
Work as set to end of Row 24.

Row 25: K1 MC, K38 in pattern, knit next 10 sts on
a piece of waste yarn. Slip these last 10 sts back onto
the left-hand needle and knit in pattern as per the chart
to last st, K1 in MC.
Fasten off CC yarns.
Work in St st until work measures 4⅜ in from end of rib,
ending with a WS row.

Fingers
Little finger: Using MC, K2tog, K8, slip next 54 sts onto a
stitch holder, cast on 2 sts, K8, K2tog. Slip these 20 sts to
dpns. Join to work in the round and knit eight rounds. Bind
off loosely. Break yarn.

Chart
MC   White Square
CC1   Dark Grey Square
CC2   Light Grey Sqaure

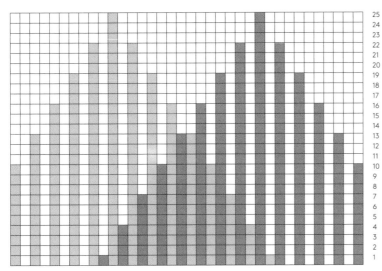

25
24
23
22
21
20
19
18
17
16
15
14
13
12
11
10
9
8
7
6
5
4
3
2
1

36 35 34 33 32 31 30 29 28 27 26 25 24 23 22 21 20 19 18 17 16 15 14 13 12 11 10 9 8 7 6 5 4 3 2 1

Ring finger: Slip next 9 sts from front of glove and 9 sts from back onto dpns. Pick up 2 sts from the cast-on edge of the little finger over the gap—20 sts total. Knit ten rounds. Bind off loosely. Break yarn.

Middle and index fingers: Work as for ring finger, picking up 2 sts from cast-on edge of previous finger.

Thumb
Using dpns, pick up the 10 sts both below and above the row of waste yarn—you will have 20 sts over 2 needles. Very carefully pull the waste yarn out, then divide the sts equally among 4 dpns. Pick up 1 st at each end of the hole—22 sts total.
Knit eight rounds. Bind off loosely.

LEFT
Work as for right, apart from Row 25:
Row 25: K1 in MC, knit 24 sts in pattern, knit the next 10 sts using waste yarn. Slip the last 10 sts just knitted back onto left-hand needle, work chart to last stitch, K1 in MC.

FINISHING

Weave in ends. If necessary, use MC to darn any small gaps that may have been left at the base of fingers. Using appropriately colored yarn, use mattress stitch to sew an invisible seam exactly 1 st in from the edge, sewing from base of little finger to bottom of rib.

FULL-FINGERED GLOVES

Use the same pattern for short-fingered gloves, but work the fingers to the following lengths (or adjust to your finger lengths as necessary):
Little finger: 2⅛ in
Ring finger: 2¾ in
Middle finger: 3 in
Index finger: 2¾ in
Thumb: 2 in

Do not bind off, but close as follows:
Fingers:
Round 1: [K2tog, K2] 5 times.
Round 2: K.
Round 3: K2tog to last st, K1.
Break yarn, draw through sts, and fasten off.

Thumb:
Round 1: [K2tog, K2] 5 times, K2tog.
Round 2: K.
Round 3: K2tog to end.
Break yarn, draw through sts, and fasten off.

MAKING CONVERTIBLE GLOVES WITH REMOVABLE MITTEN TOP

This style is adaptable for when a little more dexterity is needed. The top of the mitten and the thumb can be slid on and off as required.

Work short-fingered gloves pattern, then add the mitten top and thumb top to each glove.

Mitten Top

With dpns, starting at seam edge and four rows below start of fingers, pick up a loop from each stitch across back of hand for 36 sts, place marker, cast on 36 sts, place marker. Join to work in the round.

Rounds 1–4: Knit to marker, slip marker, work in K2, P2 rib to marker, slip marker. Work in St st across all sts until work measures 1¾ in from start of mitten top.

Shape top:

Round 1 and all odd rounds: [K1, SSK, knit to 2 sts before marker, K2tog, K1] twice.
Round 2 and all even rounds: K.

Repeat these two rounds until 36 sts remain. Graft sts using Kitchener stitch.

Thumb Top

With dpns, pick up 12 sts on the outer side of the thumb, four rows below bind-off. Cast on 12 sts and join to work in the round.

Rounds 1–4: K12, work 12 sts in K2, P2 rib.

Rounds 5–16: K.

Shape top:

Round 1: [K2tog, K2] 6 times.
Round 2: K.
Round 3: K2tog 6 times.
Break yarn, draw through sts, and fasten off.

WAVE CIRCLE SCARF

Wave was inspired by the patterns in the water in Houton Bay, Orkney. On the rare occasion when the sea is calm and flat, the wake from the nearby ferries comes into the bay in a really uniform rhythm with shallow peaks almost strobing along the surface of the water. This project takes you back to knitting flat again, required to provide a fluid drape around the shoulders and grafted to create a continuous loop. It has quite a large pattern repeat, which is uncommon in hand knitting but gives you a striking result.

Finished Size
Circumference: 53⅛ in
Width: 7⅞ in

Yarn
Jamieson's Shetland Spindrift
       3 balls *Verdigris* (**MC**)
       2 balls *Natural White* (**CC**)
Waste yarn

Needles & Notions
Pair US 2 (3mm) straight needles

Gauge
28 sts × 29 rows = 4 × 4 in

Note
When working from the chart,
odd numbered rows are knit rows
and read from right to left. Even
numbered rows are purl rows and
read from left to right.

INSTRUCTIONS
Using provisional method and waste yarn, cast on 55 sts.
Work through the chart 7 times, omitting the last row of the
final repeat to end Row 391.

FINISHING
Unravel the provisional cast-on and place the released sts on
a knitting needle. Graft the two ends using MC.
Darn over the sts with CC so that the pattern continues all
the way around the scarf. Weave in ends and block.

Chart
MC   *Grey Square*
CC   *White Square*

ICELANDIC SWEATER

This sweater is worked from the neck down, and in the round for the yoke, body, and sleeves. It is very important to check your gauge and measurements throughout. The ribbed cuffs on the sleeves are long enough to be turned up to create a snug and windproof fit around the wrists.

To Fit	Small (4–6)	Medium (8–10)	Large (12–14)
Chest circumference	34⅝ in	37⅜ in	40⅛ in
Body length (top shoulder to hem)	21⅝ in	22 in	22½ in
Neck	13 in	14⅛ in	15⅜ in
Sleeves at bicep	11⅞ in	13 in	14½ in
Sleeves at wrist	7½ in	7⅞ in	8¼ in

Yarn

Jamieson's Shetland Spindrift

11–13 balls *Heron (MC)*

3–4 balls *Poppy*

Waste yarn

Needles & Notions

US 2 (3mm) circular needle 40 in long and dpns

US 1 (2.5mm) circular needle 40 in long

Stitch holders

Stitch markers

Gauge

30 sts × 42 rows = 4 × 4 in over colorwork using larger needles

Notes

For each round, read chart from right to left, knit every round.

When choosing size, note that sweater should be worn with approximately 4 in positive ease.

When only one number is given, it applies to all sizes.

INSTRUCTIONS

Yoke

Using MC and larger needle, cast on 100 (108, 116) sts loosely. Place marker and join to work in the round. Work in K2, P2 rib for ¾ in. Knit one round.

Next round: [K2, M1] across round—150 (162, 174) sts. Knit until work measures 2 in from start of ribbing.

Next round: [K2, M1] across round—225 (243, 261) sts. Knit until work measures 3⅞ in from start of ribbing.

Next round: [K3, M1] across round—300 (324, 348) sts. Knit until work measures 5⅞ (5⅞, 6¼) in from start of ribbing.

Next round: K3 (0, 5), *M1, K4 (4, 3), M1, K5 (4, 4); repeat from * across round—366 (405, 446) sts. Knit until work measures 7⅞ (8¼, 8⅝) in from start of ribbing.

Size M only: Knit to end of round, M1—406 sts.
Size L only: [K221, K2tog] twice.

Remove start-of-round marker.

Chart
MC　　*White Square*
CC　　*Grey Square*

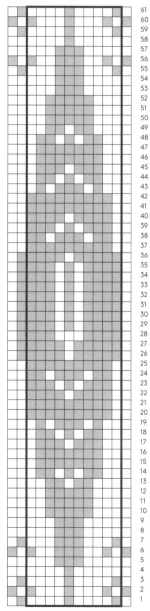

Divide Body and Sleeves

*K113 (123, 133) sts, slip next 70 (80, 90) sts to holder for sleeve, cast on 10 sts, place marker, cast on 10 sts; repeat from * across round—266 (286, 306) sts.

You will now be working the body, the front and back sts being separated by markers.

Join in CC.

*Slip marker, work first stitch of chart, work marked 10-st repeat 13 (14, 15) times, then work final 2 sts of chart.
Repeat from * once more.

Work through the 61 rounds of the chart as set, then break CC. Knit until work measures 13¾ in from underarm, or 1⅝ in short of desired length.

Next round: [K131 (141, 151), K2tog] twice—264 (284, 304) sts.

Using smaller needle, work in K2, P2 rib for 1⅝ in.
Bind off loosely.

WORKING THE SLEEVES

Transfer the held sleeve sts onto larger needle. Pick up and knit 20 sts from cast-on edge at underarm, placing marker at center of these sts to mark start of round—90 (100, 110) sts.

Knit one round.

Working marked repeat only, work chart, repeating 9 (10, 11) times across the round.

Shape the sleeve

Decrease round: SSK, knit until 2 sts rem, K2tog.

Work decrease round every 6th round, 10 (7, 18) times—70 (86, 74) sts.

Work decrease round every 4th round, 7 (13, 5) times—56 (60, 64) sts.

Knit until work measures 16⅛ (16½, 16⅞) in (or desired length) from underarm to start of ribbing.

Using smaller needle, work in K2, P2 rib for 5⅛ in (or to desired length).

Bind off loosely.

Repeat for other sleeve.

FINISHING

Weave in ends. If necessary, use MC to darn any small gaps at the underarm joins.

To wear, fold sleeve cuffs up.

LOKI SWEATER

This sweater is worked in the round from the waist up.
It has a dropped shoulder to give the body a loose fit, but the ribbed arms
are intended to fit snugly. It is very important to measure your knitting
throughout to ensure a consistent garment width in the sections of
both colorwork and plain knitting.

To Fit	Small (4–6)	Medium (8–10)	Large (12–14)
Chest circumference	38½ in	42⅞ in	40⅛ in
Body length (top shoulder to hem)	22½ in	22⅞ in	23¼ in

Yarn

Jamieson's Shetland Spindrift

11 (11, 13) balls *Dove* (MC)

3 (3, 4) balls *Natural White* (CC)

Notions

US 1 (2.5mm) circular needle
40 in long
US 2 (3mm) circular needle
40 in long
US 1 (2.5mm) circular needle
40 in long and dpns
Stitch markers
Stitch holders

Gauge

26 sts × 30 rows = 4 × 4 in over stockinette stitch using larger needle

Notes

For each round, read chart from right to left, knit every round.

When choosing size, note that sweater should be worn with up to 8 in positive ease.

INSTRUCTIONS

Body

Using MC and smaller circular needle, cast on 256 (284, 312) sts. Place marker and join to work in the round. Work in K2, P2 rib for 1⅝ in.

Change to larger needle.

Next round: Slip marker, M1, work 128 (142, 156) sts for front, place marker, M1, work 128 (142, 156) sts for back—258 (286, 314) sts.

Next round: *Slip marker, K1 in MC, work first 0 (7, 0) sts of chart, work marked 14-st repeat 9 (9, 11) times, work final 1 (8, 1) sts of chart, K1 in MC. Repeat from * once more.

Work through the 100 rounds of the chart as set, then break CC. Knit in MC only until work measures 14⅝ in from cast-on edge, or desired length up to underarm.

Front

Next round: Slip marker, K to next marker, remove marker. Place remaining sts on holder for back—129 (143, 157) sts.

Starting with a purl row, work front flat in St st for 4¾ (5⅛, 5½) in, ending with a purl row.

Next row: K49 (53, 58) and put these sts on holder for left shoulder, K31 (37, 41) sts, and put these sts on holder for the front neck, knit to end of row.

Chart
MC   *Grey Square*
CC   *White Square*

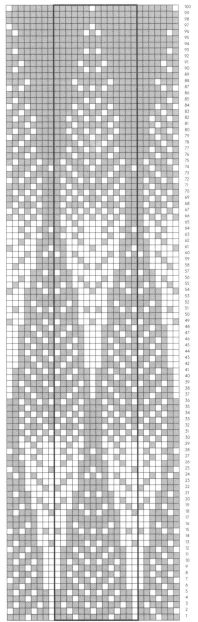

29 28 27 26 25 24 23 22 21 20 19 18 17 16 15 14 13 12 11 10 9 8 7 6 5 4 3 2 1

Right Shoulder
Next row: P.
Next row: K1, SSK, knit to end of row.

Repeat the last two rows 8 more times.
40 (44, 49) sts rem. Work in St st until work measures 7⅞ (8¼, 8⅝) in from start of armhole. Leave sts on holder.

Left Shoulder
With WS facing, return to sts held for left shoulder. P one row.

Next row: Knit to last 3 sts, K2tog, K1.
Next row: P.

Repeat the last two rows 8 more times.
40 (44, 49) sts rem. Work in St st until work measures 7⅞ (8¼, 8⅝) in from start of armhole. Leave sts on holder.

Back
Return to sts held for the back.
Work back flat in St st until work measures same as front from start of armhole.
Next row: K40 (44, 49) sts and place these sts on holder for right shoulder, K49 (55, 59) and place these sts on holder for back neck, knit to end of row. With WS facing, work a three-needle bind-off across the shoulders. Turn right sides out.

Neck
Using MC and smaller circular needle or dpns, pick up and knit 10 sts down the left side of front neck, knit across the held 31 (37, 41) sts for the front of neck, pick up and knit 10 sts up the right side of neck, knit across the held 49 (55, 59) sts at back of neck—100 (112, 120) sts

Work in K2, P2 rib for 1⅛ in. Bind off loosely in pattern.

Sleeves
Using MC and smaller circular needle or dpns, and starting at the underarm, pick up and knit 52 (54, 56) sts from each of the front and back armholes. Place marker to show start of round—104 (108, 112) sts.

Work one round in K2, P2 rib.
Next round: Work 2tog, work in pattern until 2 sts remain, work 2tog.
Next round: Work in pattern as set.
Repeat these two rounds until 68 (76, 84) sts remain.
Work in K2, P2 rib for 3⅛ in.
Next round: Work 2tog, work in pattern until 2 sts remain, work 2tog.
Work three rounds in pattern as set.

Repeat these four rounds until 40 (40, 44) sts remain.

Work in K2, P2 rib until sleeve measures 14⅝ (15⅜, 16⅛) in, or desired length from underarm. Bind off loosely.

FINISHING
Weave in ends and block.

INDEX

ACKNOWLEDGMENTS

Firstly, I would like to thank Judith Hannam and
Sophie Allen for giving me the opportunity to write
a knitting book and for all their guidance throughout
the entire process.

Caro Weiss, our amazing photographer: there are no limits
to her talent and enthusiasm no matter how muddy, cold,
or windy the location. www.caroweiss.com

Louise Barrington and Vendella Gebbie: our lovely
models who brought the knitwear to life with fun and laughs
throughout the long, chilly days shooting on location.

Sharon Stephens: our makeup artist on the shoot, who
is so skilled in bringing out the best in people. Thank you to
Sharon for looking after us all with her Mary Poppins bag
of endless supplies. www.sharonstephen.com

Sarah Moar: a retired English teacher and obsessive hand
knitter, who knitted many of the pieces in this book. Knitting
pattern instructions would often come back from Sarah
peppered with grammatical and spelling corrections—with
alternate suggestions in the margins. Thank you, Sarah!

Thank you to our other amazing knitter, Ivy Kemp.
Ivy will knit anything, no matter how big, complicated,
or difficult. She's been known to visit the local welders
to have her knitting needles extended for her more
ambitious projects!

Thank you, Jamieson's of Shetland, who provided the
beautiful 100% Shetland yarn.

Kerrie Aldo, whose beautiful handmade waxed cotton
coats were worn in the photoshoots. These coats were
perfect for keeping out the cold winds on the Orkney
cliff tops and complemented the knitted garments
perfectly. www.kerrialdo.com

RESOURCES

Yarn Brands
Jamieson's of Shetland www.jamiesonsofshetland.co.uk
Woolfolk Yarn www.woolfolkyarn.com
New Lanark Wool www.newlanarkshop.co.uk
UK Alpaca www.ukalpaca.com
Guernsey Wool guernseywool.co.uk

Knitting Shops: EU & UK
Fluph www.fluph.co.uk
Love Knitting loveknitting.com
The Quernstone, Stromness, Orkney. If you are
ever in Orkney this shop has an absolutely brilliant
selection of yarns, needles, and notions.
Ba Ram Ewe, Yorkshire baaramewe.co.uk
Loop www.loopknittingshop.com

Knitting Shops: US
Purl Soho purlsoho.com
Fancy Tiger Crafts www.fancytigercrafts.com
Fringe Supply Co www.fringesupplyco.com
Tolt Yarn and Wool www.toltyarnandwool.com

Wool Wash
Ecover Delicate Laundry Wash (available
from health food shops and supermarkets)
Soak Wash soakwash.com
Eucalan www.eucalan.com
Twig & Horn Wool Soap twigandhorn.com

Software
Knit Bird knitbird.com
Stitch Mastery www.stitchmastery.com

General
Clover Pom Pom Makers (widely available from
many craft and knitting shops)
Yarn Substitution database yarnsub.com
The Campaign For Wool www.campaignforwool.org